GARY LARSON'S THE Curse OF Madame "C"

A FAR SIDE Collection

WARNER BOOKS

A Warner Book

First published in Great Britain in 1994 by Warner Books.

The Curse of Madame "C" copyright © 1994 by FarWorks, Inc.
Cartoons Copyright © 1993, 1994 by FarWorks, Inc.

The Far Side is a cartoon feature created by Gary Larson,
syndicated internationally by Universal Press Syndicate and first
published in the United States by Andrews and McMeel.

The moral right of the author has been asserted.

A CIP catalogue record for this book
is available from the British Library.

ISBN 0-7515-1093-9

Printed and bound in Great Britain by
BPC Hazell Books Ltd
a member of
The British Printing Corporation Ltd
on Sava Pro

Warner Books
A Division of
Little, Brown and Company (UK)
Brettenham House
Lancaster Place
London WC2E 7EN

It all started many years ago. I was fresh out of college and I had decided to spend my summer backpacking across Europe.... Yes, my summer in Europe that led to my lifetime in <u>Hell</u>!

One day, as the sun began to set, I found myself in the midst of some beautiful farmlands. I probably should have stopped at one of the small, quaint villages that dotted the landscape. Alas, I kept walking...

Before long, I sensed I was in trouble. The pleasant countryside seemed to take a more sinister turn. Still, I tried to maintain a cheery attitude.

Darkness fell and fear crept into my bones. Halfway through my favorite song, I suddenly forgot the words...

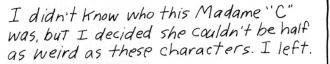

I didn't know who this Madame "C" was, but I decided she couldn't be half as weird as these characters. I left.

Oddly enough, as I started to cross the pasturelands, I found myself belting out songs I hadn't thought of for years.

It was Elvis. Back then, of course, he was still alive -- just badly drawn. He has nothing to do with my story, but I just thought I'd mention that I did see him.

I kept walking, and soon I saw a second wagon. This was the one that changed my life. (Although it was pretty cool seeing Elvis.)

A beautiful woman, also badly drawn, was at the reins. (No horse -- she was just at the reins.) I approached her wagon.

Her voice had a bewitching effect on me. Strangely enough, I also felt bothered and bewildered.

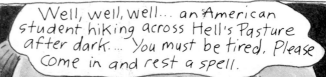

Well, well, well... an American student hiking across Hell's Pasture after dark.... You must be tired. Please come in and rest a spell.

Foolishly, I took off my glasses to get a better look at her. (Foolishly, because I actually saw better with my glasses on.)

Still, I was quickly mesmerized, and soon found myself inside her wagon. It smelled like a French barnhouse.

Would you care for a salt lick?

Okay, but only on the cheek.

A strange conversation ensued.

So, you're from the **far side** of the world, eh?

Yes, and I live on the **far side** of a small town, actually.

Oh, then summing up, you live on the **far side** of the world and on the **far side** of a small town. I find that almost interesting.

far out.

And then she leaned very close to me.

Would you care for a glass of milk?

And that's my tale. (Except for the fact that I was also bitten by a werewolf that night—but that's another story.)

I returned to my home on the **far side** of the world, and for the next several years I tried many different careers—but something kept making me move on.

I became nearly destitute. I drank too much milk. I ate too much hay. I only watched the Farm Report. Each day I wondered what was wrong with me. (At night, of course, I was a werewolf... that much I knew.)

What <u>was</u> the Curse of Madame "C"? And what <u>exactly</u> <u>did</u> that "C" stand for?...

What, indeed?.*......

* not "chicken"

The End

And so it all began....

"It's the only way to go, Frank. Why, my life's changed, ever since I discovered Stackable Livestock.®"

"... And so the bartender says, 'Hey! That's not a
soup spoon!' ... But seriously, forks ..."

"Face it, Fred — you're lost!"

"Yeah. I remember Jerry. Good friend of mine. ...
You know, I never understood a single word he said,
but he always had some mighty fine wine."

Suddenly the Mensa partygoers froze when Clarence
shockingly uttered the "D" word.

"It's a buzzard picnic, son — and you best remember
to nary take a look inside one of them baskets."

"Well, here he comes ... Mr. Never-Makes-a-Dud."

In an effort to show off, the monster would
sometimes stand on his head.

For a long time, Farmer Hansen and his tall chickens enjoyed immense popularity — until Farmer Sutton got himself a longcow.

Humboys

"Well, actually, Doreen, I rather resent being called a 'swamp thing.' ... I prefer the term 'wetlands-challenged mutant.'"

"A word of advice, Durk: It's the Mesolithic. We've domesticated the dog, we're using stone tools, and no one's *naked* anymore."

Christmas morning 1837: Santa Anna's son, Juan, receives the original Davy Crockett hat.

2ª How much wood would a woodchuck chuck if a woodchuck could chuck wood?
(a.) 250 board feet
(b.) 500 board feet
(c.) 1000 board feet

The Wildlife Management finals

"Hey, we'll be lucky if we *ever* sell this place! ...Well, it's like everyone says — location, location, location."

"My God, Carlson! After years of searching, this is an emotional moment for me! ... Voilà! I give you the Secret Elephant Breeding Grounds!"

Misunderstanding his dying father's advice, Arnie spent several years protecting the family mules.

"So George says, 'I'm goin' over there and tellin' that guy to shut that equipment off!' ... So *I* said: 'George, that guy's a mad scientist. Call the cops. Don't go over there alone.' ... Well, you know what George did."

31

In the stadiums of ancient Rome, the most feared trial was the rub-your-stomach-and-pat-your-head-at-the-same-time event.

Scotty in hell

"This is it, son — my old chompin' grounds. ...
Gosh, the memories."

"The truth is, Stan, I'd like a place of my own."

Daffy's résumé

"OK, I got one — do you say 'darn it' or 'dern it'?"

34

"Struck from behind, all right ... and from my first examination of the wound, I'd say this was done by some kind of heavy, blunt object."

"Now if you all would examine the chart, you will notice that — well, well ... seems Mr. Sparky has found something more engrossing than this meeting."

"Now watch your step, Osborne. ... The Squiggly Line people have an inherent distrust for all smoothliners."

"So let's go over it again: You're about a mile up, you see something dying below you, you circle until it's dead, and down you go. Lenny, you stick close to your brothers and do what they do."

"I *would* have gotten away scot-free if I had just gotten rid of the evidence. ... But, shoot — I'm a packrat."

"I'm sorry, Sidney, but I can no longer help you. ...
These are not my people."

Monster game shows

"So, they tell me you fancy yourself a tuba player."

Thirty years had passed, and although he had no real regrets about marrying Wendy, buying a home, and having two kids, Peter found his thoughts often going back to his life in Never-Never-Land.

The Sandwich Mafia sends Luigi to "sleep with the fourth-graders."

"Oh, Professor DeWitt! Have you seen Professor *Weinberg's* time machine? ... It's digital!"

"Well, this guidebook is worthless! It just says these people worshipped two gods: one who was all-knowing and one who was all-seeing — but they don't tell you which is which, for crying out loud!"

"It's a cute trick, Warren, but the Schuberts are here for dinner, so just 'abracadabra' this thing back to where it was."

Primitive mail fraud

The party was going along splendidly — and then Morty
opened the door to the wolverine display.

It's a known fact that the sheep that give us steel wool have no natural enemies.

"Hey! *You* don't tell *me* what makes 'er tick! *I* know what makes 'er tick, sonny boy!"

The questions were getting harder, and Ted could feel Lucky's watchful glare from across the room. He had been warned, he recalled, that this was a breed that would sometimes test him.

In medieval times, a suit of armor often served as a family's message center.

Tales of the Early Bird

"So, Professor Sadowsky, you're saying that your fellow researcher, Professor Lazzell, knowing full well that baboons consider eye contact to be threatening, handed you this hat on that fateful day you emerged from your Serengeti campsite."

For the time being, the monster wasn't in Ricky's closet.
For the time being.

"Well, I'd recommend either the chicken-fried steak or maybe the seafood platter. But look — I gotta be honest with ya — nothin' we serve is exactly what I'd call food for the gods."

"That's him. Second from the end — the 12-footer!"

"Oh, and *that* makes me feel even worse! ...
I laughed at Dinkins when he said his
new lenses were indestructible."

More tension on the Lewis and Clark expedition.

Midget westerns

Basic field trips

Moments before he was ripped to shreds, Edgar vaguely recalled
having seen that same obnoxious tie earlier in the day.

Summoned by the gonging, Professor Crutchfeld stepped into the clearing. The little caterpillars had done well this time in their offering.

"I'm sorry, sir, but the reservation book simply says 'Jason.' ... There's nothing here about Jason *and* the Argonauts."

"Today, our guest lecturer is Dr. Clarence Tibbs, whose 20-year career has culminated in his recent autobiography, *Zoo Vet — I Quit!*"

Specialized obituaries

Zeke froze. For the longest time, all he could
do was stare at the chocolate mint that
"someone" had placed on his bedroll.

"Hey! ... You!"

54

"Oh, and a word of warning about Mueller over there. ... He's got a good head on his shoulders, but it's best not to mention it."

It was an innocent mistake, but nevertheless, a moment later Maurice found himself receiving the full brunt of the mummy's wrath.

At the Insurance Agents Wax Museum

"Vera! Come quick! Some nature show has a hidden camera in the Ericksons' burrow! ... We're going to see their entire courtship behavior!"

"The dentist just buzzed me, Mrs. Lewellyn — he's ready to see Bobby now."

"I've been told you don't like my dirt!"

The Ice Crusades

"Frank ... don't do that."

Classic conversation stoppers

"OK, everyone, we'll be departing for Antarctica in about 15 minutes. ... If anyone thinks he may be in the wrong migration, let us know now."

Backing out of the driveway, Mr. Peabody suddenly brought his car to a stop. He had already heard a peculiar "thump," and now these flattened but familiar-looking glasses further intrigued him.

"No, no. ... Not this one. Too many bells and whistles."

At Electric Chair Operators Night School

A few days following the King Kong "incident,"
New Yorkers return to business as usual.

After many years of marital bliss, tension enters the Kent household.

"Well, as usual, there goes Princess Luwana — always the center of attention. ... You know, underneath that outer wrap, she's held together with duct tape."

"Look. If you're so self-conscious about it, get yourself a gorilla mask."

"Could you come back later?
He's catching a few Y's right now."

Crucial decisions along life's highway

Winning the lottery had changed his life, but at times Chico still felt strangely unfulfilled.

THE NOT FUN WHATSOEVER HOUSE

"And then one of the little kids shined his flashlight into the corner
of the basement, and there they saw these strange jars. ...
Some said 'creamy,' some said 'crunchy'... "

"It's Jim Wilkins, Dave. Same as the others. Trussed up like a Christmas present with his hunting license stuffed in his mouth. ... I want this bear, Dave. I want him bad."

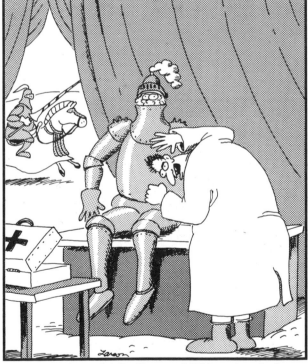

"Ooo! You're right, Sir Dwayne! If I knock right here, I can make him start buzzing. ... Ooo, and he's *angry!*"

"Well, yes, that is the downside, Fluffy. ... When we
kill her, the pampering will end."

Iggy knew he was extremely lucky
to get a room with a view.

Expatriates, they migrated in the 1920s to Paris'
Left Bank, gathering in their favorite haunts and
discussing the meaning of cream pies and big shoes.
They were, in fact, the original Boclownians.

"Care to dance, Ms. Hollings?"

It had been a wonderfully successful day, and the dugout was filled with the sound of laughter and the fruits of their hunting skills. Only Kimbu wore a scowl, returning home with just a single knucklehead.

"Oh, man! The coffee's *cold*!
They thought of *everything*!"

Douglas is ejected from the spoon band.

Fortunately, even the Boy Scouts who
fail knot-tying get to go camping.

The entire parliament fell dead silent.
For the first time since anyone could remember,
one of the members voted "aye."

Jurassic parking

Clark's mother

History shmistory

"Dang it, Morty! ...You're always showing
this picture of me you took at
7 o'clock in the morning!"

Eskimo rescue units

Primitive theme parks

"Whoa! Another bad one! ... I see your severed head lying quietly in the red-stained dirt, a surprised expression still frozen in your lifeless eyes. ... Next."

"Most interesting, ma'am — you've identified the defendant as the one you saw running from the scene. I take it, then, that you're unaware that my client is a *walking* stick?"

"It's OK! Dart not poisonous. ... Just showin' my kid the ropes!"

Once again, Vernon has a good shirt ruined by
a cheap pocket octopus.

Tension mounts in the final heat of the
paper-rock-scissors event.

PRIMATE
HOUSE

"Listen up, my Cossack brethren! We'll ride into the valley like the wind, the thunder of our horses and the lightning of our steel striking fear in the hearts of our enemies! ... And remember — stay out of Mrs. Caldwell's garden!"

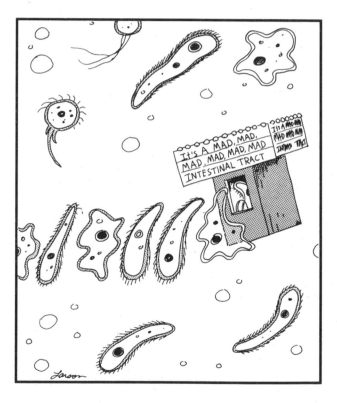

Professor Ferrington and his controversial theory that dinosaurs were
actually the discarded "chicken" bones of giant, alien picnickers.

"OK, Professor Big Mouth, we've all chipped in.
Here's the hundred bucks, but remember —
you gotta kiss her on the *lips*!"

HAVE A NICE DAY

The whole family always enjoyed the way Uncle Numanga could reach over and "find" a skull in little Tooby's ear.

CONGRATULATIONS
FRANK JOHNSON
MERRIEST MAN
OF THE MONTH

At the Vatican's movie theater

"Sorry, son, but for you to understand what happened, you have to first understand that back in the '60s we were all taking a lot of drugs."

Professor Wainwright's painstaking field research to decode the language of bears comes to a sudden and horrific end.

"Uh, let's see ... I'll try the mammoth."

"Just keep starin', buddy, and
I'll show ya my *bad* eye!"

Entomological rodeos

Vegetarian towns of the Old West

"Listen, Noreen — *you* wanna be the photographer next time, be my guest."

Ironically, Barnum's and Bailey's respective kids — Sid and Marty —
both ran away one night to join corporate America.

Vacationing from their jobs of terrorizing young teenagers, zombies will often relax at a Western dead ranch.

After being frozen in ice for 10,000 years, Thag promotes his autobiography.

"Sorry, ma'am, but your neighbors have reported not seeing your husband in weeks. We just have a few questions, and then you can get back to your canning."

"Well, I've got good gnus and I've got bad gnus."

More trouble brewing

94

"Ha! That finishes it! ... I always knew he'd
be back one day to get the other one!"

"I dunno, Andy. ... Mom said we were never to go near the old Sutter place."

"Smash your left hand down about right here three times, then twice up in this area, then three times right about here. ... That's 'Louie Louie.'"

Raymond's last day as the band's sound technician.

Before starting their day, squirrels must first pump themselves up.

"You were hit last night by some cult, Mr. Gilbert.
... Not the sickest cult I've ever seen,
but a cult nonetheless."

Dr. Frankenstein vacations in Hawaii

Bored towns of the Old West

"And down here we keep Fluffy. ...
We're afraid he may have gone mad."

Prairie dog developers

"Talk about adding insult to injury!
Not only did we arrive late, but they
deliberately left his organ-donor card."

"Time out, please! ... Eyelash!"

"Hey, you'll love it! All she needs is some gravel, a few plants, and maybe one of those miniature human skeletons."

"OK, kids, here we go. ... And I believe Danny's right, Randy — it's his turn to eat the queen."

"Whoa! ... Think I found the problem, buddy."

The first day at fly summer camp

Incredibly, Morty had forgotten to
bring a pocketbook.

Vern, Chuck, and the pope go fishing

Beverly Hills of the North Pole

Back home in his native India, Toomba tells and retells the story
of his daring escape from the Cleveland Zoo.

"Pardon me, boys — is that the
Chattanooga Iron Horse?"

"You're a right-brained sort of person,
Mr. Sommersby — *very* creative, artistic, etc. ...
Unfortunately, I think I also see why you're
having trouble figuring out your gas mileage."

"Oh, God! It's that creepy Ted Sheldon and Louis Dickerson. ... They're skinkheads, you know."

Later, when one of the monsters cranked up the volume, the party really got going.